Englisch für Minis

Die Deutsche Bibliothek – CIP-Einheitsaufnahme

Ein Titelsatz für diese Publikation ist bei
Der Deutschen Bibliothek erhältlich.

Es ist nicht gestattet, Abbildungen dieses Buches zu scannen, in PCs oder auf CDs zu speichern oder in PCs/Computern zu verändern oder einzeln oder zusammen mit anderen Bildvorlagen zu manipulieren, es sei denn mit schriftlicher Genehmigung des Verlages.

© 2002 Pattloch Verlag GmbH & Co. KG, München
Ein Unternehmen der Verlagsgruppe Droemer-Weltbild

Lektorat: Annemarie Langhammer
Umschlaggestaltung: Daniela Meyer, München,
unter Verwendung einer Illustration von Nina Broja, München
Layout und Satz: Ruth Bost, Pattloch Verlag, München
Reproduktion: Kaltnermedia, Bobingen
Druck und Bindung: Appl, Wemding
Printed in Germany

ISBN 3-629-00405-9
www.pattloch.de

Almuth Bartl • Nina Broja

Englisch für Minis

Pattloch

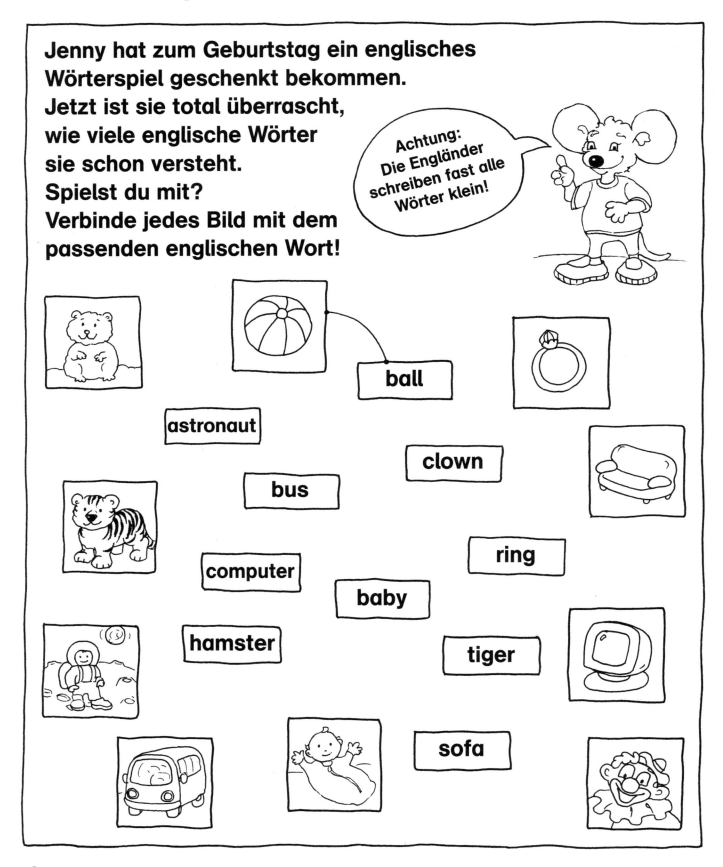

Diese Wörter sehen ein kleines bisschen anders aus als ihre deutschen Freunde. Aber verstehen kannst du sie bestimmt trotzdem.
Verbinde jedes Bild mit dem passenden Wortkärtchen!
Ergänze dann die Sätze in den Kästchen.

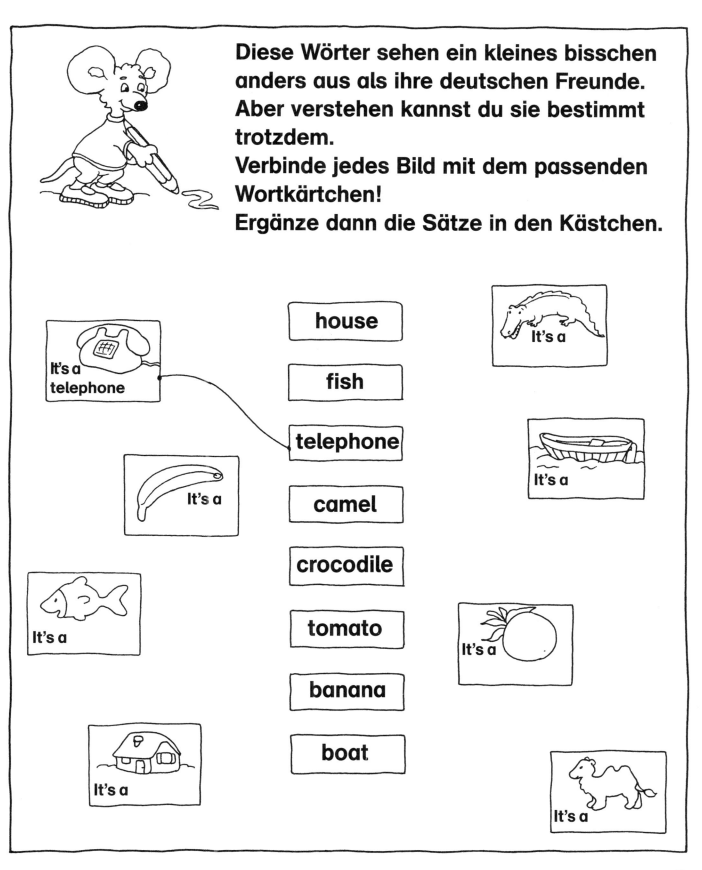

Die Farben

Male jedes Wort in der Farbe des Gegenstandes an!

Die Buntstifte

In jedem Buntstift findest du ein Farbwort.
Kreise es ein und male dann den ganzen Stift in dieser Farbe aus!

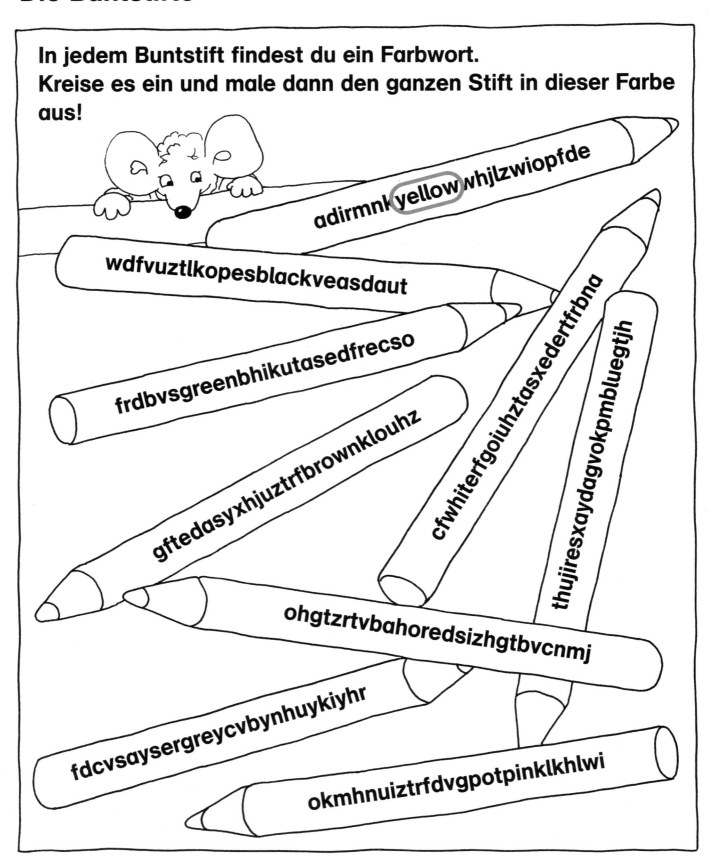

Die Zahlen

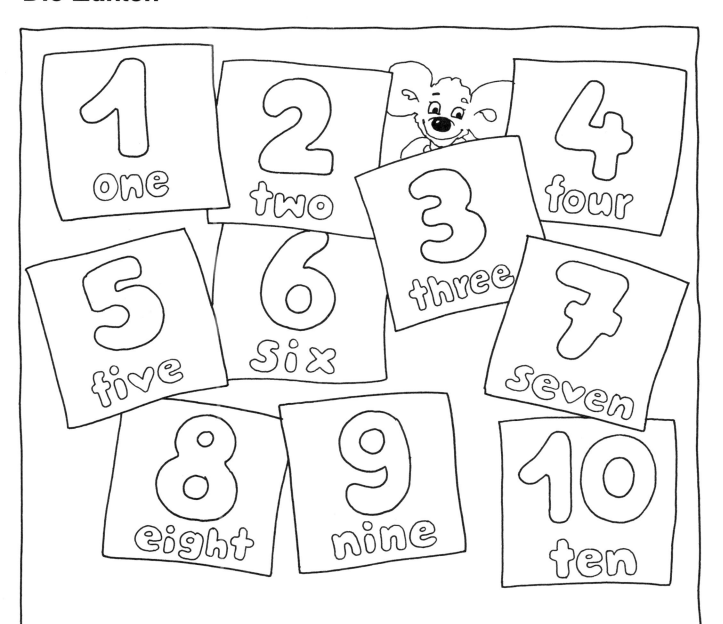

Male die Zahlen so aus:

Number eight is green.
Number four is blue.
Number one is red.
Number seven is yellow.
Number two is black.

Number six is brown.
Number three is white.
Number nine is orange.
Number ten is pink.
Number five is grey.

Richtig oder falsch?

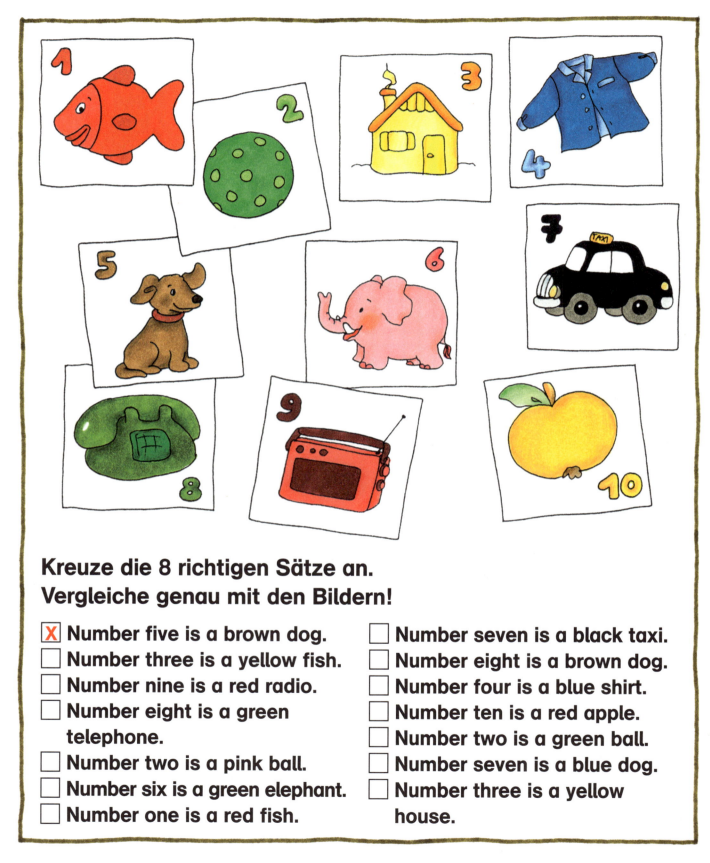

**Kreuze die 8 richtigen Sätze an.
Vergleiche genau mit den Bildern!**

- [X] Number five is a brown dog.
- [ ] Number three is a yellow fish.
- [ ] Number nine is a red radio.
- [ ] Number eight is a green telephone.
- [ ] Number two is a pink ball.
- [ ] Number six is a green elephant.
- [ ] Number one is a red fish.
- [ ] Number seven is a black taxi.
- [ ] Number eight is a brown dog.
- [ ] Number four is a blue shirt.
- [ ] Number ten is a red apple.
- [ ] Number two is a green ball.
- [ ] Number seven is a blue dog.
- [ ] Number three is a yellow house.

Zähle genau!

Von Punkt zu Punkt

Verbinde die Zahlen von 1–10!

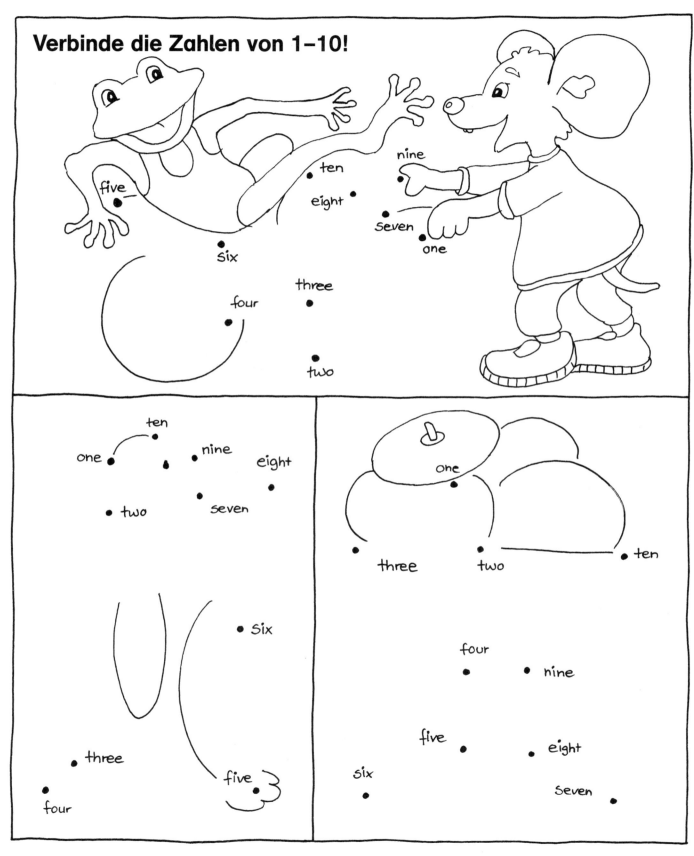

Welche Zahlen fehlen?

In jeder Reihe der Zahlenmauer befinden sich die Zahlen von 1 bis 10. Aber in jeder Reihe fehlt eine Zahl. Die sollst du suchen und in die letzten Steine eintragen.

Die Zahlenschlange

Die Schweinchen

Jenny darf den kleinen Schweinchen Namen geben. Welche sie sich ausgedacht hat, erfährst du so: Jede Zahl steht für einen Buchstaben und zwar:

1	2	3	4	5	6	7	8	9	10
J	I	E	P	L	S	G	A	Y	M

Übersetze die Zahlen in Buchstaben und du kannst die vier Namen lesen!

Tiere auf dem Bauernhof

Can you see a tiger?	☐ Yes, I can. ☐ No, I can't.	Can you see a fish?	☐ Yes, I can. ☐ No, I can't.
Can you see a hen?	☐ Yes, I can. ☐ No, I can't.	Can you see a cock?	☐ Yes, I can. ☐ No, I can't.
Can you see a horse?	☐ Yes, I can. ☐ No, I can't.	Can you see a rabbit?	☐ Yes, I can. ☐ No, I can't.
Can you see a crocodile?	☐ Yes, I can. ☐ No, I can't.	Can you see a sheep?	☐ Yes, I can. ☐ No, I can't.
Can you see a cat?	☐ Yes, I can. ☐ No, I can't.	Can you see a fox?	☐ Yes, I can. ☐ No, I can't.

Versteckte Tiere

In jeder Kiste hat sich ein Tier versteckt. Aber welches? Lies die Buchstaben ganz genau, kreise das Wort ein und kreuze das richtige Tier an!

Tiere im Zoo

11 x Yes, I can
5 x No, I can't

Betrachte das Bild genau! Lies die Fragen, die dir Jenny stellt, und kreuze dann die richtigen Antworten an!

Can you see a camel?	☐ Yes, I can. ☐ No, I can't.
Can you see a pig?	☐ Yes, I can. ☐ No, I can't.
Can you see a zebra?	☐ Yes, I can. ☐ No, I can't.
Can you see a monkey?	☐ Yes, I can. ☐ No, I can't.
Can you see a horse?	☐ Yes, I can. ☐ No, I can't.
Can you see an elephant?	☐ Yes, I can. ☐ No, I can't.

Can you see a giraffe?	☐ Yes, I can. ☐ No, I can't.	Can you see a crocodile?	☐ Yes, I can. ☐ No, I can't.
Can you see a frog?	☐ Yes, I can. ☐ No, I can't.	Can you see a duck?	☐ Yes, I can. ☐ No, I can't.
Can you see a penguin?	☐ Yes, I can. ☐ No, I can't.	Can you see a lion?	☐ Yes, I can. ☐ No, I can't.
Can you see a cow?	☐ Yes, I can. ☐ No, I can't.	Can you see a bear?	☐ Yes, I can. ☐ No, I can't.
Can you see a tiger?	☐ Yes, I can. ☐ No, I can't.	Can you see a snake?	☐ Yes, I can. ☐ No, I can't.

Das Tierwörter-Rätsel

**Nenne jedes Tier bei seinem Namen!
Suche dann die passenden Buchstaben und male sie farbig aus!**

Wenn du alles richtig machst, ergeben die übrigen Buchstaben in jeder Zeile ein Wort.

lhaimomner

czearbrorta

erleadphiaont

gihoratffeel

crboucosdile

hsanamstkeer

22

Lies genau!

Zu jedem Bild passt nur eine Beschreibung. Kreuze sie an!

Die Kleidung

Bunte Kleider

Große Wäsche

Jenny hat fast alle ihre Anziehsachen gewaschen und auf die Wäscheleine gehängt. Hake im linken Kasten alle Kleidungsstücke ab, die an der Leine hängen! Am Ende weißt du, welches Kleidungsstück noch im Wäschekorb liegt. Schreibe den englischen Namen auf den Korb!

Jennys Wohnzimmer

Auf dieser Seite siehst du die Gegenstände aus Jennys Wohnzimmer noch einmal. Suche zu jedem Bild das passende Wort und streiche beides durch! Wenn du alles richtig machst, bleibt am Schluss ein Wort übrig. Male das dazu passende Bild ins leere Kästchen!

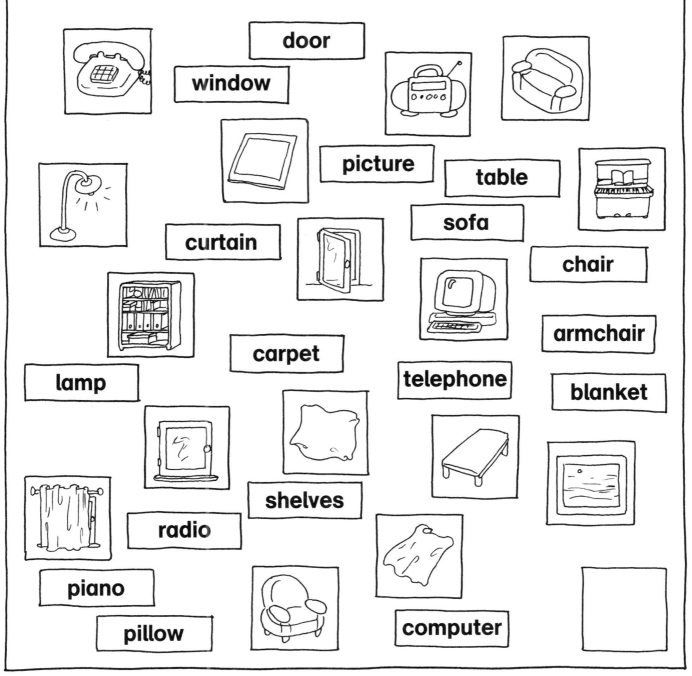

Vokabel-Quiz

**Neben jedem Bild kannst du drei Wörter lesen.
Aber natürlich passt nur eines.
Kreuze es an!**

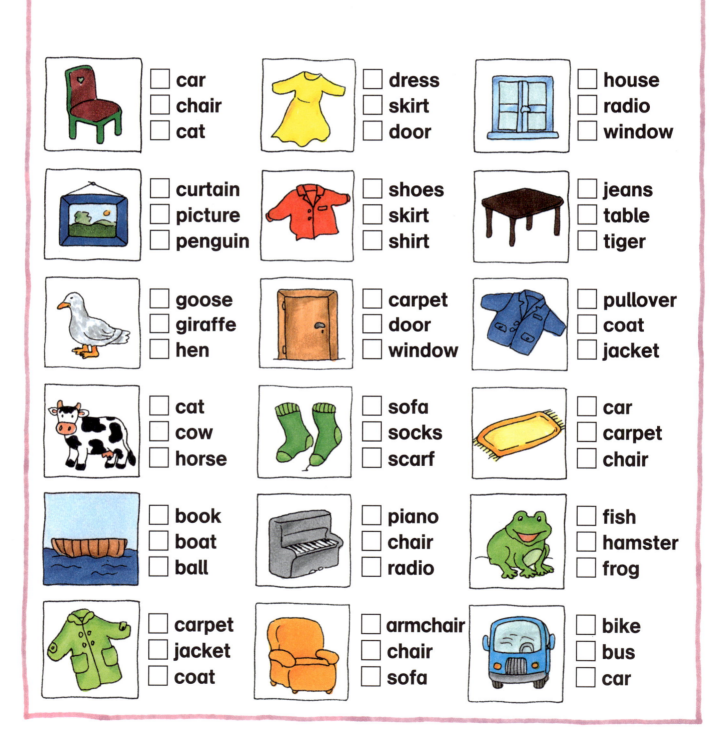

Jennys Familie – Jenny's family

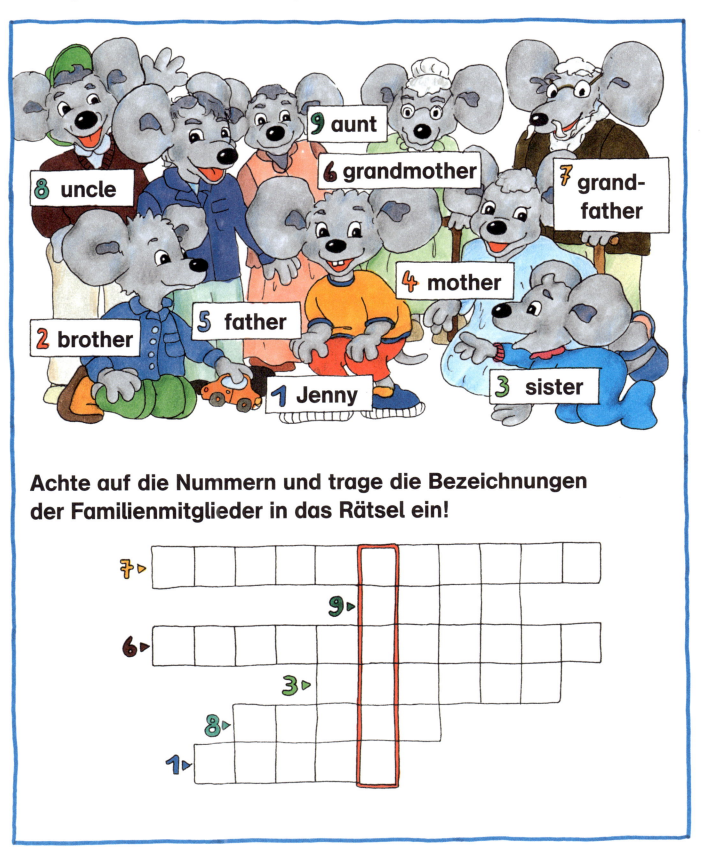

Achte auf die Nummern und trage die Bezeichnungen der Familienmitglieder in das Rätsel ein!

Jennys Wörterquatsch

Nur in zehn Kästchen stimmen Wort und Bild überein. Streiche alle anderen durch!

book	bus	fish	ball
frog	radio	table	lamp
pillow	carpet	car	elephant
book	curtain	shorts	shirt
sister	window	giraffe	hand
chair	skirt	ring	hamster
dog	hat	grandmother	camel

Die Luftballons

Jenny und ihre Freunde haben eine Menge Luftballons. Immer vier Wörter auf den Ballons gehören zur gleichen Gruppe. Ein Wort passt nicht zu den anderen. Streiche es durch!

Ja oder nein? Schreib den Satz zu Ende!

Die Körperteile

Verbinde alle roten Wortkärtchen mit den passenden Körperteilen!

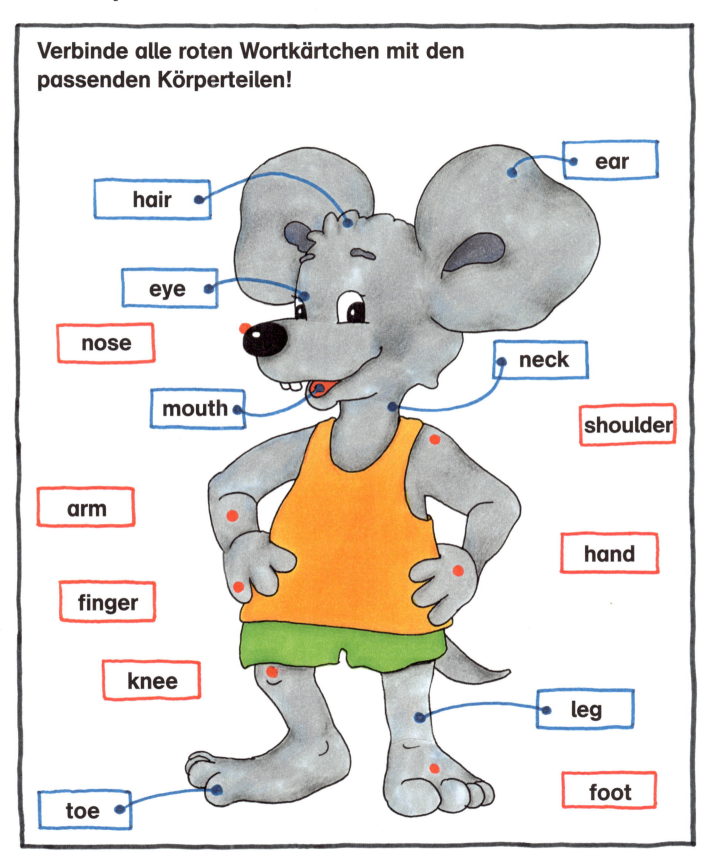

Auf dem Markt

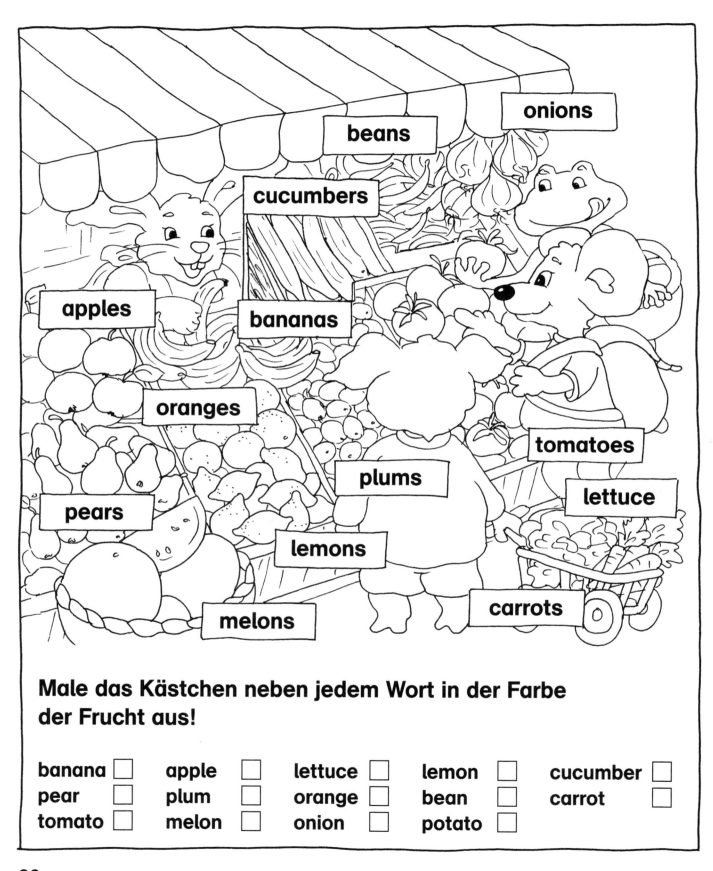

Male das Kästchen neben jedem Wort in der Farbe der Frucht aus!

banana ☐	apple ☐	lettuce ☐	lemon ☐	cucumber ☐
pear ☐	plum ☐	orange ☐	bean ☐	carrot ☐
tomato ☐	melon ☐	onion ☐	potato ☐	

Frische Ware

Gerade kommt der riesige Laster mit frischem Obst und Gemüse auf dem Markt an. Findest du heraus, was er alles geladen hat?

Guten Appetit!

Jenny hat für sich und ihre Freunde den Tisch gedeckt. Aber leider hat sie nicht nur Essbares auf den Tisch gestellt.
Streiche schnell die vier Dinge durch, die man besser nicht essen sollte!

Schau genau!

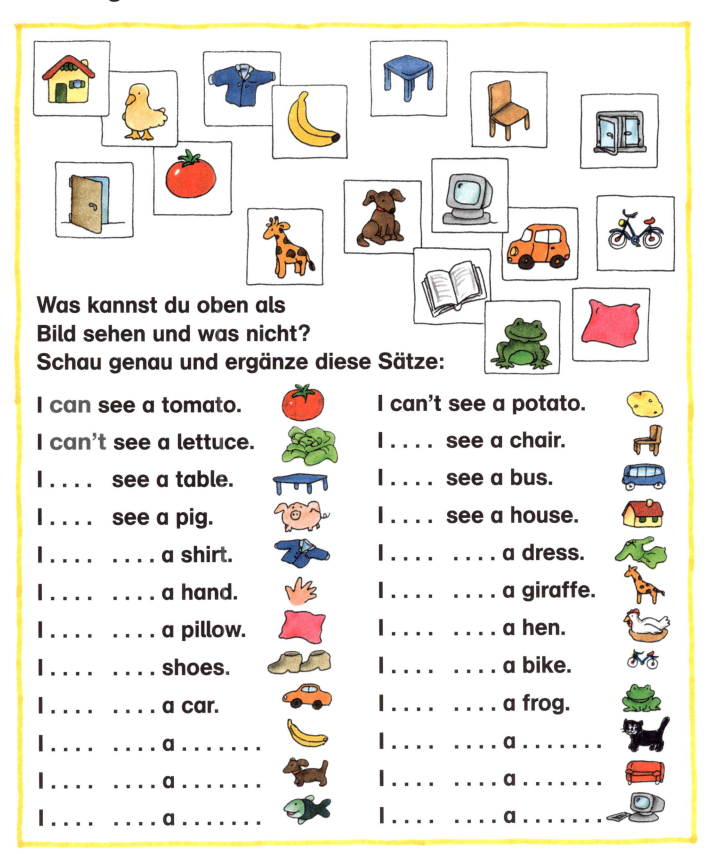

Was kannst du oben als Bild sehen und was nicht? Schau genau und ergänze diese Sätze:

I can see a tomato.
I can't see a lettuce.
I . . . . see a table.
I . . . . see a pig.
I . . . . a shirt.
I . . . . a hand.
I . . . . a pillow.
I . . . . shoes.
I . . . . a car.
I . . . . a . . . . .
I . . . . a . . . . .
I . . . . a . . . . .

I can't see a potato.
I . . . . see a chair.
I . . . . see a bus.
I . . . . see a house.
I . . . . a dress.
I . . . . a giraffe.
I . . . . a hen.
I . . . . a bike.
I . . . . a frog.
I . . . . a . . . .
I . . . . a . . . .
I . . . . a . . . .

39

Die Küche

In jeder Zeile ist ein Wort versteckt. Kreise es ein!

hbkiztdefröpijk**fork**vdsaklöm

gtfrscvlouj**stove**lkoupztrewfi

asdf**plate**fvgbhuiokmjhgtrmn

okjhztrfdeghjkl**refrigerator**kil

hbgvfcderewasexylkiol**knife**o

hnbgfrti**spoon**klttfrdcbhuoutz

hnbvgfcdsxsmklöäou**bowl**jhti

panklkiuztgtfrdcxvgtzleoxfew

oiutghbgdaölyhst**bucket**kiujhz

hgvf**bottle**dskiitzgffrdbnjmklok

hgbnymylaokdjuetwgbdjd**glass**

gsthunbsfspiu**cup**lkjhutzgfvnjas

gfdresaswasquz**basket**zuopoujik

zhgtrfr**ubbish**lkbinhgtrfdesvwal

Ja oder nein?

Schau genau und ergänze dann die Sätze!

Is this a dog?
Yes, it is.

Is this a cow?
No, it isn't.

Is this a chair?
Yes, ...

Is this a car?
No, ...

Is this a bottle?
. . . . , ...

Is this a spoon?
. . . . , ...

Is this a shirt?
. . . . , ...

Is this a bowl?
. . . . , ...

Is this a fork?
. . . . , ...

Is this a sheep?
. . . . , ...

Is this a picture?
. . . . , ...

Is this a refrigerator?
. . . . , ...

Is this a plate?
. . . . , ...

Is this a window?
. . . . , ...

Is this a pot?
. . . . , ...

Is this a knife?
. . . . , ...

Is this a banana?
. . . . , ...

Is this a potato?
. . . . , ...

Is this a basket?
. . . . , ...

Jennys Wörterrätsel

Jenny hat sich ein spannendes Wörterrätsel
für dich ausgedacht.
Folge genau Jennys Anweisungen!
Wenn du alles richtig machst, bleibt am Schluss
ein Wort übrig. Kreise es mit einem roten Stift ein!

- Streiche alle Wörter,
  die mit e enden!
- Streiche alle Farbwörter!
- Streiche alle Tiernamen!
- Streiche alle Wörter mit
  vier Buchstaben!

house
dog
yellow
blouse
pig
blue
nine
shoe
hair
brown
bike
green
goose
black
monkey
three
cow
nose
four
door
camel
pink
elephant
red
duck
frog
book
table
coat
cat
hen
fish
one
pear
star
white
bean
ring
horse
mouse
ball
five
rabbit
foot
zebra
grey
giraffe
bowl
radio
boat
hand

43

So viel zu tun!

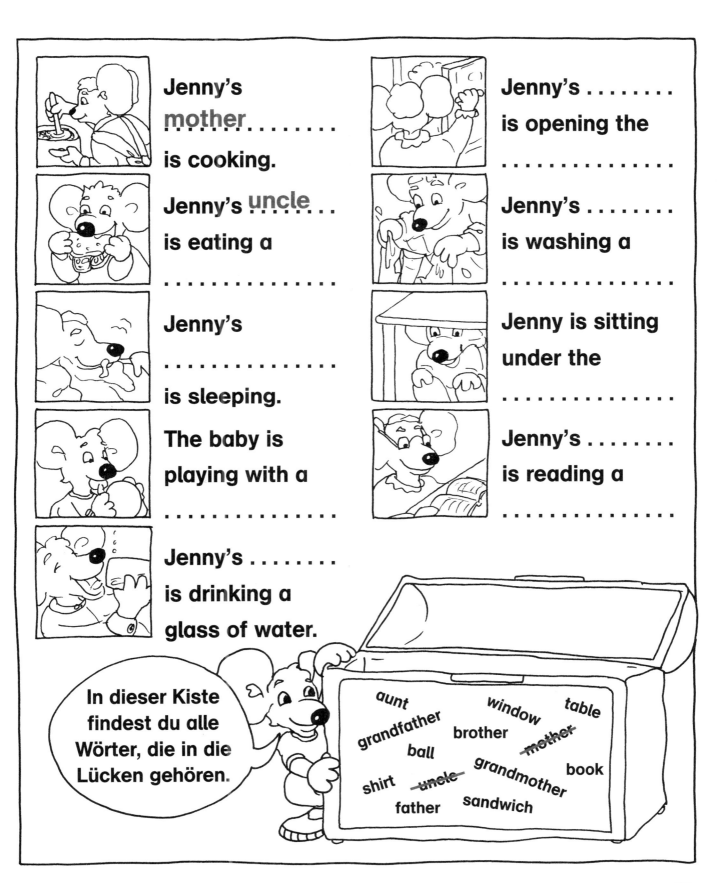

Jennys Schlafzimmer

Streiche in jedem Satz zwei falsche Wörter durch!

in   on   under

	The duck is ~~in~~ ~~on~~ under the chair.		The ball is in on under the bed.
	The cup is in on under the table.		The baby is sitting in on under the floor.
	The pig is in on under the box.		The computer is in on under the wardrobe.
	The car is in on under the wardrobe.		The frog is in on under the basket.
	The shoes are in on under the table.		The bird is in on under the lamp.
	The bag is in on under the chair.		Jenny is in on under the bed.

Das Kreuzworträtsel

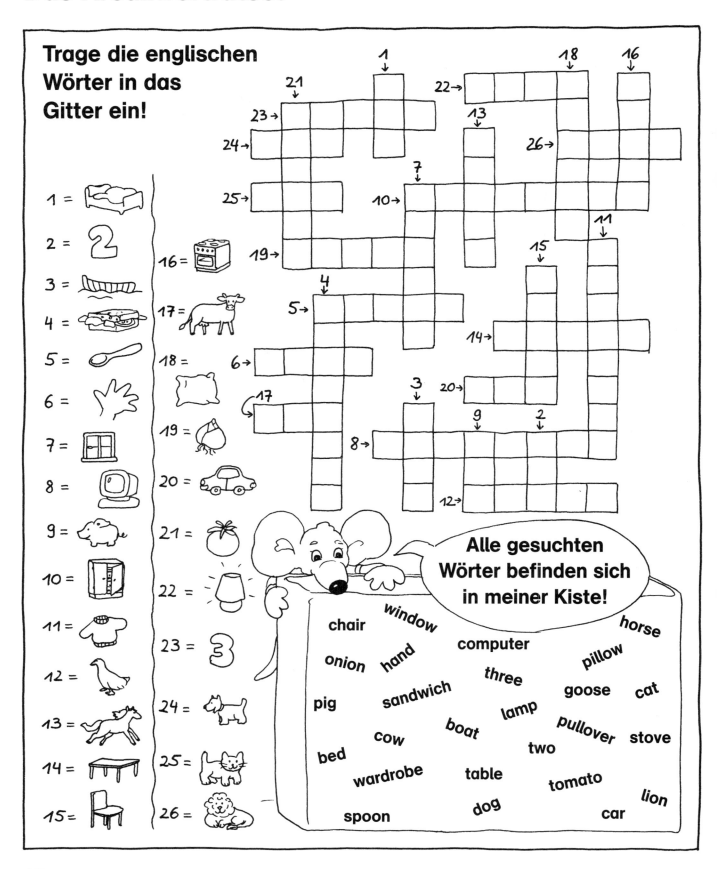

Davor und dahinter

in front of · behind

Ergänze in jedem Satz entweder in front of oder behind!

The rabbit is
....
the car.

The pig is
....
the box.

The frog is
....
the sofa.

The chair is
....
the table.

Schreibe unter jedes Bild das passende Wort:
in • on • under • behind • in front of

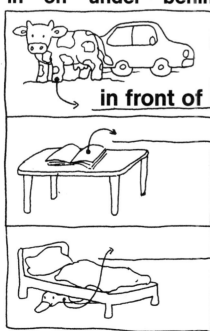
in front of

In der Schule

Beantworte die Fragen mit: Yes, she has.   Yes, he has.
No, she hasn't.   No, he hasn't.

Has Jenny got a satchel?   Yes, she has.
Has Jenny got a calculator?   No, she hasn't.
Has Billy got a satchel?   Yes, he has.
Has Billy got a book?   No, he hasn't.
Has Jenny got a sandwich?   . . . . , she . . . .
Has Billy got a banana?   . . . . , he . . . .
Has Jenny got a pencil case?   . . . . , ...
Has Jenny got a rubber?   . . . . , ...
Has Billy got a pencil?   . . . . , ...
Has Billy got a ruler?   . . . . , ...
Has Jenny got a book?   . . . . , ...
Has Billy got a pen?   . . . . , ...
Has Jenny got a book?   . . . . , ...
Has Billy got a carrot?   . . . . , ...
Has Jenny got a sponge?   . . . . , ...
Has Jenny got a pear?   . . . . , ...
Has Billy got a pair of scissors?   . . . . , ...
Has Jenny got a ruler?   . . . . , ...
Has Billy got a rubber?   . . . . , ...

Einzahl und Mehrzahl

one pencil	two pencils	one book	two books
	hands		
one sheep	three sheep	one foot	two feet
one fish	four fish	one tooth	many teeth

Welcher Satz passt genau?

**Kreuze neben jedem Bild den Satz an,
der genau dazu passt!**

☐ Jenny is writing a letter.
☐ Jenny is playing with two balls.
☐ Jenny is eating a sandwich.

☐ Two cows are behind the house.
☐ Three rabbits are playing ball.
☐ Three rabbits are sitting on the sofa.

☐ Two pigs are in the boat.
☐ Two rabbits are in the boat.
☐ Two pigs are in the car.

☐ The dog is washing the pig.
☐ Jenny is washing the dog.
☐ Jenny is sleeping in the bed.

☐ Jenny is drinking a glass of water.
☐ The frog is drinking a bottle of water.
☐ The frog is drinking a glass of water.

☐ Jenny's grandmother is reading a book.
☐ Jenny's grandfather is writing a book.
☐ Jenny's grandfather is reading a book.

Das neue Schweinehaus

Peggy Schwein hat sich ein neues Haus gebaut und hat auch schon eine Menge Sachen in das neue Haus geräumt. Findest du alle 18 Dinge? Kreise sie ein!

house
househouse
housesofahouse
househousehousehouse
housechairhousehousebedhouse
househousehousetablehousehousehouse
housespoonhousehousepothousehouseho
househousehousestovehousehousehouseh
househousearmchairhousehousehousehou
sehousehousehousehousebowlhouse
househouseplatehouseknifehousehou
sehousehousehousehousehoushelvesh
househousepicturehousehousehouseh
ousehousehousecuphousehousehouse
houseballhousehousehousehousecarpethous
ehousehousepillowhousehousehousehouseh
ousehousehousehousehouseblanketho

54

Wie spät ist es?

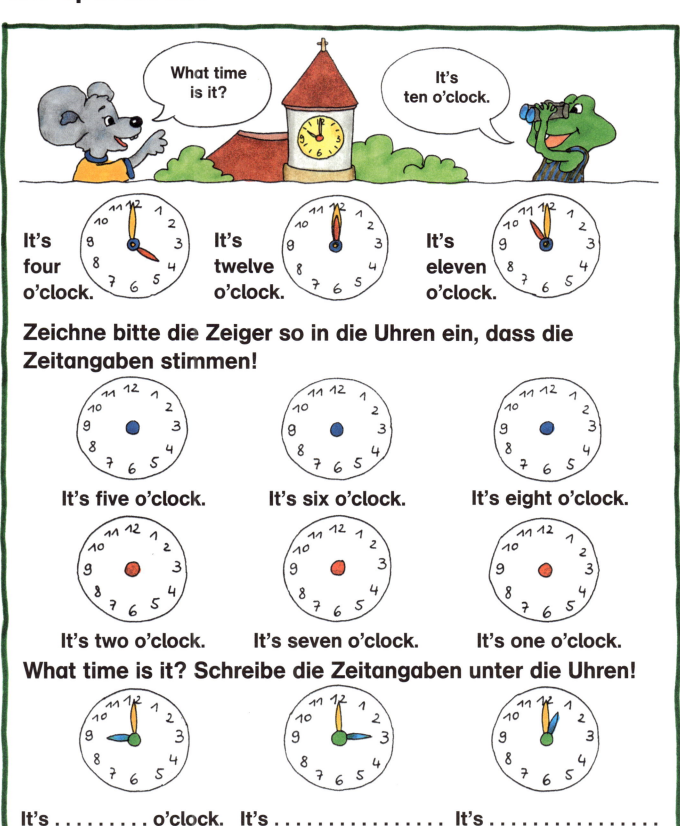

It's four o'clock. It's twelve o'clock. It's eleven o'clock.

Zeichne bitte die Zeiger so in die Uhren ein, dass die Zeitangaben stimmen!

It's five o'clock. It's six o'clock. It's eight o'clock.

It's two o'clock. It's seven o'clock. It's one o'clock.

What time is it? Schreibe die Zeitangaben unter die Uhren!

It's . . . . o'clock. It's . . . . It's . . . .

Am Strand

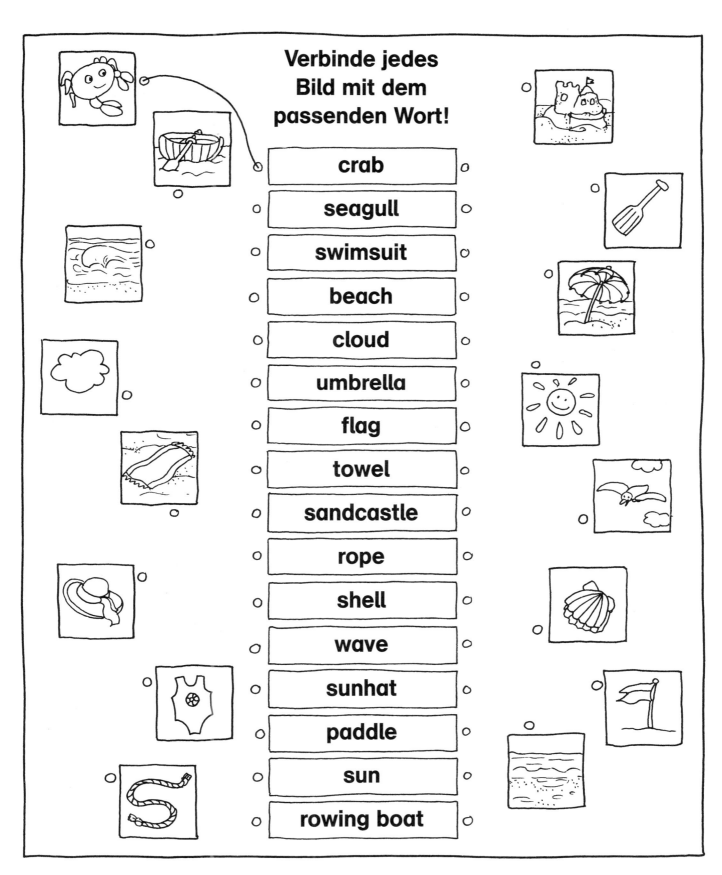

Jennys Speiseplan

Schreibe auf, was Jenny in dieser Woche so alles isst!

On	Monday	Jenny eats	carrots.
On	....	Jenny eats	....
On	....	Jenny eats	....
....		eats	cornflakes.
....		eats	....
....		eats	....
....		eats	cake.

Peggy und Billy

Peggy und Billy wollen verreisen und haben ihre Koffer gepackt. Schau genau nach, wem die Dinge gehören, und schreibe Sätze!

This is Billy's   flag.   It's his flag.

This is Billy's   radio.   It's . . . . radio.

This is Peggy's shirt.   It's her shirt.

. . . .

. . . .

. . . .

. . . .

. . . .

. . . .

. . . .

. . . .

Wir reimen

Verbinde immer zwei Wörter, die sich reimen!

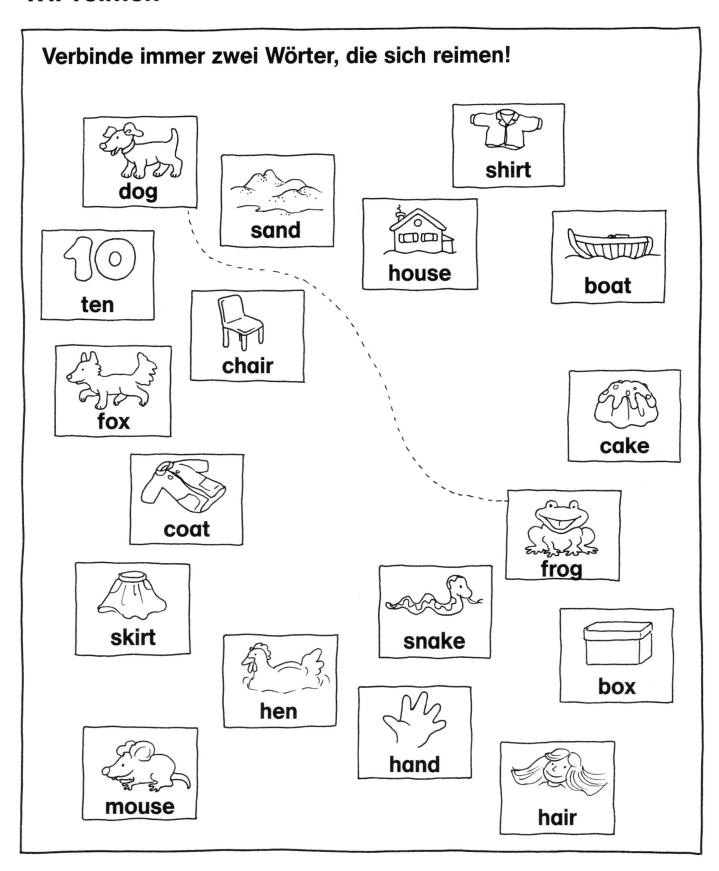

Wortregister

A
a – ein, eine
apple – Apfel
arm – Arm
armchair – Sessel
astronaut – Astronaut
aunt – Tante

B
baby – Baby
banana – Banane
ball – Ball
bag – Tasche
basket – Korb
beans – Bohnen
bed – Bett
behind – hinter, dahinter
bird – Vogel
black – schwarz
blackboard – Tafel
blanket – Decke
blue – blau
boat – Boot
book – Buch
bottle – Flasche
blouse – Bluse
bowl – Schale
box – Kiste
boy – Junge
brother – Bruder
brown – braun

bucket – Eimer
bus – Bus
butter – Butter

C
chair – Stuhl
cake – Kuchen
calculator – Taschenrechner
camel – Kamel
car – Auto
carpet – Teppich
carrot – Karotte
cat – Katze
cloud – Wolke
coat – Mantel
cock – Hahn
computer – Computer
cook – kochen, der Koch
cornflakes – Cornflakes
cow – Kuh
crab – Krabbe
crocodile – Krokodil
cucumber – Gurke
curtain – Vorhang
cup – Tasse

D
dog – Hund
door – Tür
drink – trinken, das Getränk
dress – Kleid
duck – Ente

E
eat – essen
ear – Ohr
egg – Ei
eight – acht
elephant – Elefant
eye – Auge

F
father – Vater
finger – Finger
fish – Fisch
five – fünf
flag – Fahne
floor – Fußboden
foot – Fuß
fork – Gabel
four – vier
fox – Fuchs
Friday – Freitag
frog – Frosch
in front of – vor, davor

G
giraffe – Giraffe
girl – Mädchen
glass – Glas
gold – Gold
goose – Gans
grandfather – Großvater
grandmother – Großmutter
green – grün
grey – grau

H
hand – Hand
hair – Haar, Haare
hamster – Hamster
hammer – Hammer
hat – Hut
he – er
hen – Henne
her – ihr
his – sein
horse – Pferd
house – Haus

I
I – ich
in – in
in front of – vor, davor
is – ist
it – es

J
jacket – Jacke
a pair of jeans – Jeans

K
kitchen – Küche
knee – Knie
knife – Messer

L
lamp – Lampe
leg – Bein
lemon – Zitrone
lettuce – Salat
lion – Löwe

M
map – Landkarte
melon – Melone
milk – Milch
Monday – Montag
monkey – Affe
mother – Mutter
mouth – Mund
my – mein

N
name – Name
neck – Hals
nine – neun
nose – Nase

O
on – an, auf
one – eins
onion – Zwiebel
open – offen, öffnen
orange – Orange, orange

P
paddle – Paddel
a pair of . . . . – ein Paar . . . .
pan – Pfanne
pear – Birne
pen – Füller
pencil – Bleistift
pencil case – Federmäppchen
penguin – Pinguin
piano – Klavier
picture – Bild

pig – Schwein
pillow – Kissen
pink – rosa
pizza – Pizza
plate – Teller
play – spielen
plum – Pflaume
popcorn – Popcorn
pot – Topf
pullover – Pullover
pupil – Schüler, Schülerin

R
rabbit – Hase
radio – Radio
read – lesen
red – rot
refrigerator – Kühlschrank
ring – Ring
rope – Seil
rowing boat – Ruderboot
rubber – Radiergummi
rubbish bin – Abfalleimer
ruler – Lineal

S
sand – Sand
sandcastle – Sandburg
sandwich – belegtes Brot
satchel – Schultasche
Saturday – Samstag
scarf – Schal
a pair of scissors – Schere
seagull – Möwe

63

seven – sieben
she – sie
sheep – Schaf, Schafe
shell – Muschel
shelves – Regal
shirt – Hemd
shoes – Schuhe
a pair of shorts – kurze Hose (Shorts)
shoulder – Schulter
sister – Schwester
sit – sitzen, setzen
six – sechs
sky – Himmel
skirt – Rock
sleep – schlafen
snake – Schlange
socks – Socken
sofa – Sofa
spoon – Löffel
sponge – Schwamm
star – Stern
steak – Steak
stove – Herd
sun – Sonne
Sunday – Sonntag
sunhat – Sonnenhut
swimsuit – Badeanzug

T
table – Tisch
taxi – Taxi
teacher – Lehrer, Lehrerin

telephone – Telefon
ten – zehn
the – der, die, das
three – drei
Thursday – Donnerstag
tiger – Tiger
toast – Toast
toe – Zehe
tomato – Tomate
towel – Handtuch
Tuesday – Dienstag
two – zwei

U
umbrella – Schirm
uncle – Onkel
under – unter

W
wardrobe – Kleiderschrank
wash – waschen
wave – Welle
Wednesday – Mittwoch
white – weiß
window – Fenster
worm – Wurm

Y
yellow – gelb

Z
zebra – Zebra